No Easy Answers: Our Digital World

by Gordon West

PEARSON

Glenview, Illinois • Boston, Massachusetts • Chandler, Arizona
New York, New York

ISBN-13: 978-0-328-88119-2
ISBN-10:   0-328-88119-8
1 2 3 4 5 6 7 8 9 10 V0B4 20 19 18 17 16

Contents

Life
in the
Digital
Age

The digital world, thanks in part to the explosive growth of the Internet, has transformed every aspect of our lives. The pace of technological change is astonishing. Today there's an amazing array of devices at our disposal. And there's an equally amazing variety of innovative software and applications, or apps, to run on them.

As a result, it's easier than ever for us to communicate with one another, share information, educate and express ourselves, form communities based on common interests, get work done, solve problems, and just have fun.

However, technological change doesn't always represent progress. It's important to understand that advances in technology come with risks. Rushing to adopt the latest digital trend before evaluating both its benefits and its costs could have consequences in the future—no matter how unintended they might be. For example, we all love our smartphones. But do their effects on our brains mean that these "smart" devices are actually making us less smart? The public is fascinated by driverless cars. But are these cars really better for drivers? Social media sites have opened up new ways for us to form friendships and communities, but does our reliance on social media harm our social skills?

A healthy and vibrant society requires that its citizens be informed and engaged. The same is true for the digital world. Therefore, we must ask ourselves some important questions and confront some complex issues if we are to successfully navigate our way through the digital world.

Are smartphones making us less smart?

Many people today own smartphones, and it's not hard to understand why. These pocket-sized supercomputers make it easier to connect with people, organize and find important information, get work done, and have fun. No one doubts the conveniences that smartphones have brought to our lives. However, despite these benefits, our reliance on these "smart" devices is not making us smarter.

Smartphone Culture

It's important to think about how smartphones affect our brains, considering that smartphone usage continues to rise each year in the United States—especially among young people.

Smartphone Ownership in the U.S., 2015

64% of Americans own a smartphone.

73% of Americans ages 13 to 17 have access to a smartphone.

93% of American smartphone owners ages 18 to 29 use their smartphones to avoid boredom.

Source: Pew Research Center

A New Age of Intelligence

Many proponents of the digital world assert that smartphones have revolutionized the way we think and use our brains. In an instant, we can find an answer to almost any question, no matter how important or insignificant it is. We can keep up with global events as they unfold right before our eyes. If we want to learn about a new culture or a new recipe, it's just a click or swipe away on a Web site, podcast, or app. We can carry hundreds of books on a single, lightweight device. We never have to worry about remembering directions or getting lost.

Computing Power

The most powerful supercomputer in the world is about four times faster and can hold 8.5 times more data than the human brain. Computers excel at multitasking, or doing multiple calculations and tasks at the same time. However, a computer is less efficient when it comes to learning new information. It also requires a great deal more energy to function.

7

Brain Boosters

Smartphones help our minds in a number of significant ways. They certainly are better at storing and recalling information than we are. Our brains are rather good at remembering chunks of information. But they're not totally reliable. Memories can change over time or, in some cases, fail completely.

In addition, offloading less important information and tasks to our smartphones means that our minds can deal with more complex problems and issues. By not having to memorize directions to a new store or the phone numbers of all our family and friends, we free up some valuable space in our already crammed brains.

It certainly seems as if the digital world we inhabit helps our brains. All this information easily available at our fingertips can only make us smarter, right?

Devices of Mass Distraction

Over the past few years, scientists and researchers have been studying the different ways that digital devices affect the human brain. The results aren't encouraging. The research suggests that smartphone use can lower cognitive performance, interfere with memory formation, and affect the way we communicate with each other.

At the University of Southern Maine in Portland in 2014, researchers conducted a study about the effects of mobile phones on people's abilities to perform complex mental tasks. In the study, subjects were asked to perform a simple task that involved crossing out numbers that matched a target number. Subjects also performed a similar but more complex task. Some people were asked to put away their mobile phones. Other people were told to keep their mobile phones on the table because they would be asked some questions about their phones as part of the study.

The researchers compared how the subjects with their mobile phones performed on the tasks in relation to how the subjects without their phones performed on the same tasks. They discovered that the people who had their phones out on the table performed about 20% worse on the tasks than the people who did not keep their phones out.

Most people might admit that mental performance is adversely affected when using a smartphone and trying to complete another task. But the shocking fact is that the researchers saw a decrease in mental performance with just the *presence* of a mobile phone.

Memory-Making Mischief

Smartphones affect more than just our problem-solving skills. Erik Fransén is a researcher at KTH Royal Institute of Technology in Stockholm, Sweden. He has been studying how online time affects the brain's working memory. This is what most of us know as short-term memory.

The human brain's working memory can hold only a handful of information at one time. It also needs quiet time, away from distractions, in order to process short-term memories. Fransén's research shows that a brain exposed to just a normal session of social media browsing can get overwhelmed by too much information. "And when you try to store many things in your working memory, you get less good at processing information," says Fransén.

So constant checking of e-mail, texts, and social media updates on a smartphone may, in fact, be interfering with the brain's ability to process information and form memories.

Lowering Language Skills

Our mobile phones may be convenient for keeping in touch with family and friends, but some research also indicates that texting leads to poor grammar, especially among young people.

Drew Cingel, a researcher in media, technology, and society, thinks that the shortcuts and omissions that make up "text-speak" can harm a student's grammar skills. In 2012, he administered a grammar test to middle school students in central Pennsylvania. Then the

students completed a survey about how often they texted and how often they used shortcuts and other elements of text-speak. Researchers working with Cingel reviewed the data. They concluded that the more students used text-speak when texting, the worse they performed on the grammar test.

Cingel's work indicates that our online communication may affect the way we communicate offline. The shortcuts, abbreviations, and other tricks we use when texting are likely contributing to poor spelling and grammar skills.

How U.S. Smartphone Owners Ages 18 and Older Feel About Their Devices, 2015

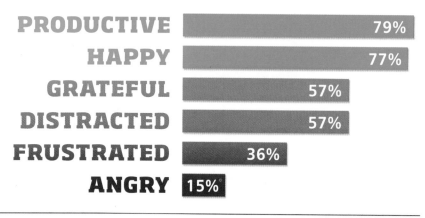

PRODUCTIVE	79%
HAPPY	77%
GRATEFUL	57%
DISTRACTED	57%
FRUSTRATED	36%
ANGRY	15%

Source: Pew Research Center

A Nation Preoccupied

Smartphone owners themselves seem to confirm what science and research indicate. For example, a Pew Research Center study conducted in 2014 and 2015 asked smartphone owners how they felt about their devices. The data in the graph indicate that a majority of people said that their phones make them more productive and happy. But more than half of those surveyed also thought that their phones were a distraction.

Our brains clearly are distracted in the presence of our smartphones. This can have dangerous effects, such as auto accidents caused by distracted drivers, decreased work productivity, and hazards to our mental health and well-being.

Smart Users

As the scientific research indicates, our smartphones have serious impacts on our brains. A smartphone can cause enough of a distraction to impair the brain's ability to concentrate on tasks as well as form memories. In addition, our real-world communication skills may be suffering as a result of the way we interact online.

More and more people are enjoying the benefits of owning and using smartphones. So it's important for us to consider how these "smart" devices influence our minds. It's up to all of us to use our devices wisely. This means spending time away from our smartphones. Our brains will be thankful.

Are streaming services bad news for musical artists?

As more people use streaming services to listen to music, a popular subject of debate has become the effect of these services on musicians. The collective outcry of many artists over the unfairness of digital streaming services has received a good deal of publicity lately. Despite this negative attention, a closer look reveals that these streaming services actually benefit artists—and listeners—in a number of important ways.

No Free Music

Some people assume that if a streaming service is free, then the artists do not get paid for their work. No one would argue that artists shouldn't be compensated for their work, and the fact is that there's no such thing as a free streaming service.

Music streaming services fall into two main categories: subscription and ad-based. Subscriptions require a monthly or annual fee to stream music; ad-based services do not require fees, but listeners hear ads every now and then while streaming music. Both models bring in revenue. This is used in part to pay royalty fees to the people who compose and record the music. So artists, in fact, get paid one way or another.

Follow the Listener

Music streaming services have grown exponentially in recent years. It's where the listeners are going, and the money too. In 2015, revenues in the U.S. from streaming services surpassed $1 billion for the first time. A majority of listeners are now receiving their music digitally.

Most streaming services pay artists based on the number of times a song is played or streamed. Subscription services generally pay more per song. Therefore, with a growing audience of listeners, even the relatively small fees from streaming services can result in a steady stream of royalties for artists. The more people hear an artist's music, the more his or her income potentially will increase.

Radio Pays Zilch

In evaluating what's fair compensation, it's important to remember that AM/FM radio stations don't pay performers anything to play their songs. The radio industry's argument for decades has been that performers are duly compensated by the exposure. Satellite radio services do pay royalties to artists, which generally come from fees charged to listeners.

Something's Better Than Nothing

Artists and other critics of streaming services may complain that artists don't get paid enough. But with streaming services, at least artists get paid something. No one can argue that streaming music is worse than the alternative that many listeners resort to, which is pirating music. Piracy is the unauthorized copying of digital content given away for free or at lower than market price. Even sharing unauthorized copies of music files with friends is considered piracy. And when listeners engage in piracy, artists receive nothing.

Digital Piracy Rates Among Americans by Age, 2013

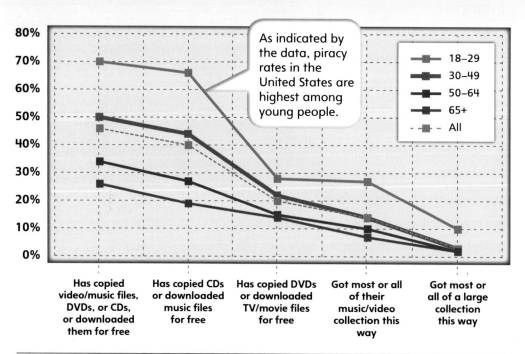

Source: The American Assembly at Columbia University

Streaming services are a huge benefit because they're getting listeners to pay for music again. Piracy rates have actually begun to fall in the United States since 2013. Both subscription and ad-based streaming services saw significant revenue growth from 2013 to 2014. Taken together, this means musical artists are getting paid now for music that used to be illegally downloaded and shared.

Better Distribution and More Exposure

Artists generally make very little from streaming services. However, streaming represents a more efficient form of music distribution and can provide good exposure for independent or struggling artists. Most artists make money by touring. So this exposure helps with their financial compensation.

Traditional forms of music distribution, usually involving physical media, are costly in terms of both time and money. Vinyl records must be pressed, compact discs printed, and everything packaged and sold to stores. These costs are generally passed on to consumers.

Streaming Stats

According to a 2015 report by the International Federation of the Phonographic Industry (IFPI), 41 million people around the world used subscription services in 2014. Millions more used ad-based streaming services.

Today, streaming services make it much easier for artists to get their music out to the public, which increases their exposure—as well as the royalty fees! As a result, streaming services offer wide-ranging exposure to artists in every genre. Country, hip-hop, jazz, folk, and uncategorized artists all have a place within the music-streaming realm. Radio play is a big part of exposing audiences to certain artists. But it's only effective for already popular or hot up-and-coming artists that the record companies are promoting. Many talented artists never get radio play because they don't fit into the specific format (country, pop, hip-hop) of a particular station. Indie artists in particular seldom get airplay outside of streaming services.

A Wealth of Information for Artists

One exciting aspect of streaming services is that they allow artists to interact with their fans and listeners in new ways. Many streaming services have built-in features that allow listeners to comment on songs and send messages to artists. They allow the artists to reply directly to their fans. Many artists have used streaming platforms to release new music or never-before-heard live performances as special gifts to fans and listeners.

Streaming services don't just allow artists to interact directly with fans. They also have the power to provide data about listening patterns: the songs that are being streamed the most or the least, the ages or geographic locations of those listening, and the times of day people are streaming. Streaming services collect an astonishing variety and amount of information about listener habits

With this information at their disposal, artists can better understand their listeners and are able to make smarter choices about recording, producing, and delivering their work.

Embracing the Future

Artists shouldn't fear that online streaming marks the downfall of the music industry. Instead, they should recognize that streaming is their future. It brings in revenue over longer periods of time than traditional CD sales. It offers exposure to millions of listeners worldwide that might not otherwise be available. And streaming is proving to be the preferred way for today's consumers to get their music.

Music-streaming services are a work in progress. Some changes will no doubt occur as these services become major players in the music-delivery business. The bottom line is that if artists want to get their music out to the largest audience, streaming services are going to play a big role in making that happen. And that could turn out to be really *good* news for artists.

Does modern technology enhance family life?

Smartphones, tablets, and other digital devices are often a source of friction for today's families. "Stop playing that game and do your homework!" and "Put down your phone when I'm talking to you!" are common refrains in many of our households. Arguments about the use of digital devices are so common that many people wonder whether technology enhances or poses serious challenges to family relationships. Some might rush to answer that modern-day devices definitely bring too many distractions that weaken family life. However, digital devices actually strengthen family life in a number of ways.

Bringing Extended Families Closer Together

In large countries such as the United States, it's no surprise that many relatives don't live close to each other and therefore gather infrequently. Not so long ago, many grandparents and grandchildren who lived far apart saw each other only on special occasions.

20

Communication with extended family members was limited to cards and letters and long-distance phone calls, which were infrequent due to their expense. Calls to relatives who lived far away had to be short and to the point!

However, today's technology provides rich opportunities for us not only to stay in touch with relatives, but also to develop deeper relationships. Kids can bond with their grandparents when they video-chat. Or they can share news about what's going on in their lives and at school on social media. Aunts and uncles can get ongoing updates on the birth and development of newborn nieces and nephews. Cousins who see each other only once in a while can regularly play online games together and stay connected via all kinds of social media. In this regard, modern technology has been a huge beneficial change for our families. In fact, a 2012 Pew Research Center study found that the main reason people over the age of 50 use social networking sites is to stay in touch with family.

Daily Family Communication

Only a generation ago, managing the daily family schedule could be a real challenge. Everyone had to plan their days in advance to figure out who needed to be where at what time, to coordinate meal times, and to manage after-school activities. Parents had to call the school office to relay a message to their children about a change in plans. Outside of school, children had to have coins and find a working payphone to let parents know where they were going to be. For some parents, receiving an outside call at work was frowned upon or even impossible. Often, family members wouldn't know who would be home for dinner or even at what time dinner would be. Missed calls and sudden changes in plans often upset the family apple cart, resulting in frustration and worry.

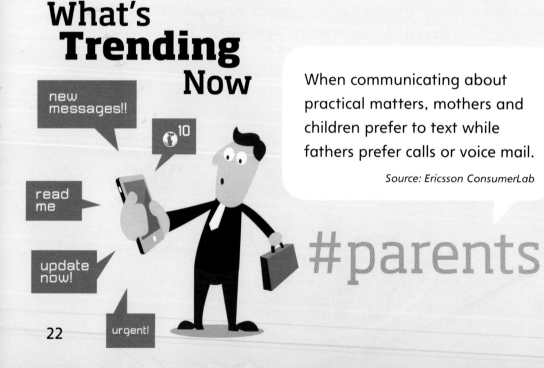

What's
Trending
Now

new messages!!

10

read me

update now!

urgent!

When communicating about practical matters, mothers and children prefer to text while fathers prefer calls or voice mail.

Source: Ericsson ConsumerLab

#parents

Modern technology has changed all of that, and for the better. Daily communication among family members is easier now than it's ever been. Today, texts and messaging apps and services help parents and children share, discuss, and schedule their daily calendars. Transportation to and from school and other activities can be handled smoothly using our smartphones and other devices.

Recent research supports this idea. According to another 2012 Pew Research Center study, more than half of adults in the United States between the ages of 18 and 49 who use mobile phones said that their devices made it easier to plan and schedule their daily routines. A 2015 study, undertaken by the technology corporation Ericsson, shows an even greater percentage. It reports that 82% of parents agree that communication technology has made logistics planning much easier. Family interactions about schedules that once might have been stressful are now easier.

A quarter of families say that even when they are all at home, they regularly use devices to communicate with each other.

Source: Ericsson ConsumerLab

#rushhour

Text message volume and online traffic soar between 6 A.M. and 10 A.M.

Source: The New York Times

#fam

Quality Time

One of the biggest complaints about how technology affects family life is that our devices can be a huge distraction. According to a 2011 University of Cambridge study, many parents think that their children's use of computers and smartphones interferes with family time.

The study also found that many children feel that their parents, aided by their devices, disrupt family time by continuing work at home. In a 2015 AVG Digital Diaries study, 54% of children worldwide said they felt their parents spend too much time checking their devices.

The good news is that families can use a variety of strategies to reduce the less desirable effects of modern technology on family life. One easy strategy many families use is to keep devices away from the table at mealtime. Setting time limits or established times for device use also helps families minimize tension and ease concerns about too much "screen time." Another successful strategy is to use modern technology to bring the family together, by playing digital games as a group or watching videos and programs everyone enjoys. In short, families can take positive steps to offset the potential negative consequences of technology.

By providing new ways for families to form and develop lasting bonds, and aiding in daily communication, technology clearly enhances family life. As for concerns about whether our devices have a negative effect on family life, it's important for families to take matters into their own hands by setting boundaries and finding opportunities to use technology together. In this regard, the key issue that families need to confront is one of control: Our devices don't control our families; our families control our devices. Modern technology is here to stay, and it will strengthen family life in a variety of ways. How we choose to use it is up to us.

Are driverless cars really an improvement over cars with human drivers?

From the moment Ford's first Model T™ came off the assembly line, people have been enamored with the power and glamour of the automobile. We love to ride in cars for enjoyment. Many of us rely on vehicles to provide transportation from one place to another. But there are just too many cars on the road today. The resulting auto accidents cause injuries and take lives. Not to mention that insurance, maintenance, and fuel can add up to major costs. And the open road loved by so many drivers is more often than not clogged with terrible traffic that pollutes the environment and makes driving more of a pain than a pleasure.

As a response to these problems, automakers have begun to develop cars that drive themselves without any human assistance. These autonomous, or driverless, vehicles are heralded as the future of auto travel around the world, and they likely are because this technology offers significant improvements over cars designed for human drivers.

While driverless cars are a relatively new development, many Americans have already formed opinions about them. In a recent survey conducted by the University of Michigan, Americans were mostly positive about the new technology.

A Safer Way to Travel

As of 2012, car accidents were the ninth leading cause of death in the world. In the United States, more than 37,000 people died and 2.35 million were injured or disabled as a result of auto accidents in 2015. A majority of accidents are caused by driver error due to such things as carelessness, driving under the influence of alcohol or drugs, and distracted driving.

In the six years that Google has been testing its driverless cars, only 16 accidents have occurred. And none of these accidents were caused by the technology, but by the humans who were riding in the cars at the time.

Removing the Human Factor

Human error is the main cause of most road accidents. This problem is virtually eliminated by driverless cars. "The autonomous car doesn't drink, doesn't do drugs, doesn't text while driving, doesn't get road rage," says Bob Lutz, vice chairman of General Motors. Lutz's company is developing a partially self-driving car for use on highways with a goal of launching in 2017.

Driverless cars are a significant improvement over cars with drivers because they are programmed to obey every law of the road—to the letter. They make full stops at stop signs, keep a safe distance behind other cars, and stick to the speed limit. The same can't be said for a majority of drivers today!

> ### "Auto-nomous"
>
> Driverless cars are not technically driverless. The cars are controlled by computers that use sensors, radar, and cameras to navigate safely on roadways. Many of these cars are still in their experimental stages, but experts predict fully autonomous vehicles will be available to the public at some point in the future.

Safe, but Not Too Safe

Some people worry that driverless cars will lead to problems on roads shared with human drivers. These critics claim that some human drivers will drive more recklessly than ever, knowing the driverless cars will not get in their way. Another issue might be the cautiousness of driverless cars. One such car being tested, for example, was stuck at a four-way intersection. Its sensors picked up movements of human-driven cars that didn't make full stops. The car refused to budge until it was completely safe. Auto experts and researchers, however, agree that these problems will be worked out with improved technology—and with fewer human drivers on the road.

Improving Quality of Life

New driving patterns brought about by driverless cars will have a positive impact on the quality of our lives. As they become more popular, these cars will change the face of towns and cities. While some people will want to own their own cars, many others will rent or lease them on a regular basis. These mobile service vehicles will offer something like a blend of car sharing and taxi service. The vehicles will pick you up at home, drive you to work, and pick you up to take you home at the end of the workday.

With more people sharing cars, there will be fewer cars on the road. That will mean less congestion and less pollution. Mobile service cars will almost always be on the road and only parked when not in use. This will mean less need for parking spaces and lots. With reduced traffic, streets and highways might be made narrower. Space will open up, especially in the cities, to provide for wider sidewalks and bike lanes, as well as more pedestrian malls and parks. The quality of life may vastly improve for millions of people around the world.

Greater Mobility for the Masses

Another benefit of driverless cars is that people who cannot drive for a variety of reasons will have greater mobility. About 25% of the U.S. population is unable to drive due to factors such as disabilities, age, and the high cost of owning a vehicle. Many more citizens will be able to travel wherever they need to go and at a fraction of the cost of a taxi or car service.

Multitudes of people will embrace the driverless service. Others will insist on owning their own driverless auto. And still others will not want to give up the pleasure and independence of driving themselves. While driverless cars may become the norm, it is unlikely that they will completely replace human drivers for some time. At some point, however, it's likely that human drivers will be ostracized from the road.

Highest Traffic Delays per Commuter, per Year, for U.S. Cities with Populations of 3 Million or More in 2015

Washington, D.C.	82 hours
Los Angeles	80 hours
San Francisco	78 hours
New York City	74 hours
Boston	64 hours

Source: USA Today

The Gift of Time

Another great benefit of driverless cars is that they will allow us to make better use of our time. Americans who commute by car to jobs in major cities waste many hours each year stuck in traffic. Driverless cars are expected to help reduce traffic, resulting in shorter commute times.

That's not the only benefit, however. In a car that drives itself, we are freed to put commuting time to more productive use. We can relax, read, use electronic devices that would be a distraction if we were driving, or even do some work before arriving at the office. One model has front-facing seats that can swivel back to help create a mobile workspace for up to four passengers. Its developer, Andre Sharpe of Regus, says, "This innovative car will change wasted time into productive time."

A New Road Ahead

Without a doubt, many of the challenges and problems we face on the road today will be solved when driverless cars replace those operated by humans. As more driverless cars move from the test roads to the open highways, we'll have a better idea of how the technology will improve our lives. Several years of development have indicated that driverless cars are far safer and can improve the quality of life for all of us.

Is social media destroying our social skills?

Many of us are familiar with the following scene: Two teens sit across from each other in a coffee shop, silently sipping their drinks. They do not talk to each other. Instead, they are staring at their devices, scrolling through newsfeeds full of their friends' pictures and status messages.

The virtual communities of social media have allowed us to connect in amazing ways. But now that social media has taken over our lives, face-to-face interactions are going the way of the dinosaur. As a result, our social skills may soon be extinct too.

Social Cues

It's hardly surprising that there's a strong correlation between social media use and a weakened ability to understand social cues. Social media does not promote face-to-face interaction. We're communicating, but in a limited way—one that includes few words and excludes facial expressions, gestures, and tone of voice.

However, social cues such as expressions and tone are crucial to gauging other people's emotions and reacting appropriately. For example, suppose someone texts you the message "That's OK, don't worry about it." Then imagine hearing a friend speak these same words to you in person, in a disappointed tone, as tears well up in her eyes. How much of the real message do you miss by relying on words alone? Face-to-face communications are filled with important cues that social media interactions lack.

The Proof Is in the Study

In 2014, psychologists at the University of California, Los Angeles, conducted a study on the relationship between digital media use and social skills. They found that an increase in digital media use can affect our ability to understand social cues. Researchers studied how well two groups of children could read nonverbal emotional cues. The first group was sent to a nature camp for five days and cut off from social media. The control group continued with its usual social media diet. Both groups were tested for their reactions to social cues before and after the five-day period. Children in the group that was cut off from social media improved their ability to read nonverbal cues significantly more than children in the control group.

It's not easy to read social cues online. We tend to communicate in artificial ways on social media. For instance, instead of "That's OK, don't worry about it," you're likely to get "That's OK! Don't worry about it!" followed by a smiley-face emoticon, even if the person typing those words feels lousy. That's because the unspoken rules of social media are different from those of in-person communication. In person, we may try to hide our feelings and appear more upbeat than we feel. But our expressions and tone often give us away. On the other hand, when we type our communications, we can hide any hint of negativity in favor of exclamation marks and smiley faces.

The Hollowness of Perfection

There may be a link between social media use and dissatisfaction with life. All that positivity is at least partly to blame. No one has a perfect life, but it can seem as if others do based on what they share. When you start to believe that all your social media friends are happier than you, you can end up feeling alone, and you may find it hard to share your reality with other people.

Sometimes all that positivity can even make you question what's real. Let's say you and some friends go to the same party. Someone later posts photos on a social media site of beaming faces and captions that include the words "amazing!" and "incredible!!" When you see the posts, you don't recognize the party as the same one you attended. *That* party was not incredible. (In fact, it was downright boring.)

You don't ask your friends what they really thought about the party because you don't want to be a downer. Instead, you "like" the party posts and respond with lots of smiley-face emoticons.

When people do express negative emotions online, they tend to be extreme about those as well. On social media, if someone isn't very, very happy, he or she may well be very, very angry. In fact, it seems that anger is the most "viral" emotion on the Internet. With the protection of anonymity, some people feel free to make hateful comments that they would never express face to face. Psychologists point out that cyberbullies, for example, engage in extreme behavior online because they don't feel responsible for their actions.

That's OK! Don't worry about it! :)

How Emotions Move Through Social Networks

In 2013, researchers at Beihang University in Beijing, China, studied how emotions spread through online communities. The diagram below is a visualization of a social network. Each dot in the diagram represents an individual, and pathways between the dots represent the online connections between individuals. The colors represent different emotions: anger, joy, sadness, and disgust. They spread at different speeds through the network, with anger clearly dominating.

　　Online haters, ranters, and fanatics are apt to lose the ability to share their feelings and opinions in person without alienating all those around them. Social media is

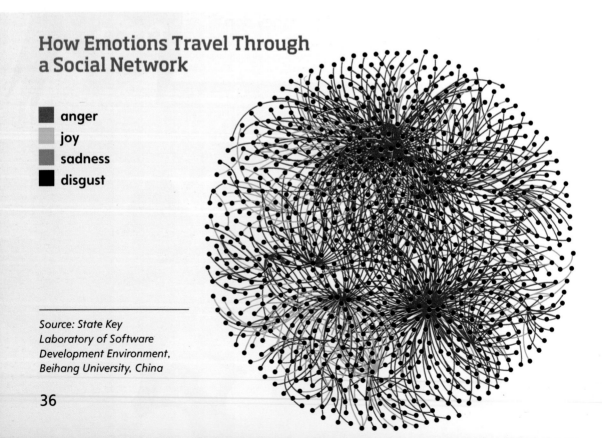

How Emotions Travel Through a Social Network

- anger
- joy
- sadness
- disgust

Source: State Key Laboratory of Software Development Environment, Beihang University, China

based on the idea of sharing. But people using social media quickly forget how to listen and respond to others—the very foundation of sharing. This affects all of us, both personally and as a society.

Who Are You?

It can be challenging enough sometimes to reconcile our *own* online personas with our real-life selves. But attempting to reconcile our friends' online and real-life selves can leave us baffled. Your social media friend may seem nothing like the same friend you know in real life. Cue more awkwardness when you happen to bump into her!

The trend toward online over real-life communication may have serious consequences for young people, in particular. The development of social skills is crucial to personal and professional satisfaction as an adult. Psychologists fear that online communication might be preventing young people from learning these skills.

Tweens and teens face enough challenges as it is. How can we help them reap the rewards of social media without putting their social skills in jeopardy? The answer, as with many things, is balance. Social media can be a wonderful communication tool. However, it should never replace face-to-face interactions. Excessive use of this tool should be curtailed as well, to allow time for other valuable activities. At the end of the day, we all need to turn off our devices and focus on our real, offline lives.

Are video games bad for you?

Ever since kids started destroying invaders from space using digital cannons or racing through a maze to avoid deadly ghosts, adults have been asking the same question: Are video games bad for young people? Chances are, if you're among the 72% of American teens who play video games, you'll answer, "What? No way!" Of course, your parents or teachers might have a different response.

Average Time Each Day Spent Among 8- to 18-Year-Olds in U.S., 1999–2009

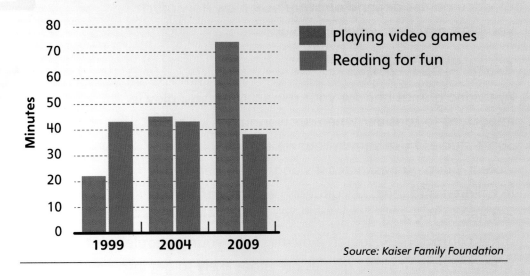

Source: Kaiser Family Foundation

    The average time teens spend playing video games daily has been increasing steadily each year. However, time spent on other leisure activities has either decreased or remained the same. This is not surprising, given the widespread availability of different gaming platforms: consoles, smartphones, computers, and tablets. So it's a smart gaming strategy to understand that video games negatively affect people's health.

Food for Thought

Over the past couple of decades, a lot of time, money, and brainpower has gone into studying what happens to children and teens when they play video games. What does that research reveal? Dr. Tom Hummer of the School of Medicine at Indiana University sums up his findings this way: "Asking what are the effects of video games is like asking what are the effects of eating food. Different games do different things." Using Dr. Hummer's food analogy, you might say that the effects of video games depend on *what* you play, *how much* you play, and even *when* you play.

Keep This in Mind

Are video games bad for your mind? *What* you play is important to consider when answering this question. Some studies have shown that repeatedly playing violent video games increases aggressive behavior in children and teens. In general, violent games are defined as those in which the player can harm or kill other characters. Research indicates that young people who play violent video games are more likely to get into arguments or physical fights than kids who do not play such games.

In a 2003 study on violent video games, Craig Anderson and co-author Douglas Gentile note that in violent video games, players take on the roles of aggressive characters. Based on their research, Anderson and Gentile conclude that because gamers are repeatedly rewarded for being aggressive in a fantasy video game world, some think that it's acceptable to use aggression to solve problems in real life.

And there is a strong appetite among American gamers for games that contain violence. If you've ever bought a video game, you're probably familiar with the rating categories by the Entertainment Software Rating Board (ESRB). The ESRB provides ratings for video games according to age appropriateness and content. In the United States, 37.5% of the top-selling video and computer games in 2014 were rated M (Mature), meaning they may contain "intense violence, blood and gore." Statistics don't show exactly who in a household is playing M-rated games. But we do know that these games are present and available.

Ratings of Top-Selling Video and Computer Games in U.S., 2014

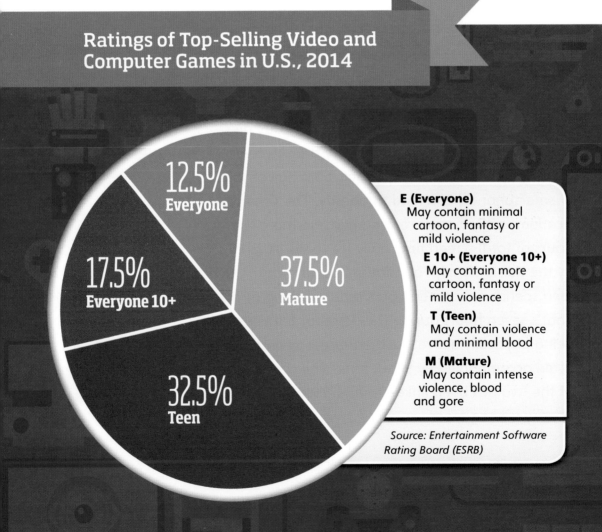

12.5%
Everyone

17.5%
Everyone 10+

37.5%
Mature

32.5%
Teen

E (Everyone)
May contain minimal cartoon, fantasy or mild violence

E 10+ (Everyone 10+)
May contain more cartoon, fantasy or mild violence

T (Teen)
May contain violence and minimal blood

M (Mature)
May contain intense violence, blood and gore

Source: Entertainment Software Rating Board (ESRB)

Body of Proof

Are video games harmful to your body? That depends on *how much* you play. Believe it or not, physical therapists have a name for a hand injury caused by repeatedly playing video games: gamer's thumb. People who have gamer's thumb experience pain and swelling in their thumb joint because of repeatedly pressing the tiny buttons on controllers. Additionally, gamers may experience aches and pains due to hunching over a smartphone or sitting at a computer for long periods of time.

Doctors are also concerned that a steady diet of screen time—that is, any activity that involves looking at a TV, computer, tablet, gaming console, or smartphone—can lead to obesity. The American Academy of Pediatrics recommends no more than two hours of total screen time daily for teens. A 2010 study by the Kaiser Family Foundation found that the average teen spends over seven hours a day looking at a screen. That's seven hours during the day that teens are not being physically active. Furthermore, screen time is often accompanied by snack time. The combination of the two has been linked to high blood pressure and obesity among teens.

The Buddy System

The verdict on video games isn't completely negative, however. *When* you play can have a positive effect on relationships. Parents might worry that sitting in front of a screen will turn their kids into loners. Yet research shows that teens, especially boys, actually use video games as a way to spend time with their friends. More than 40% of teen boys report playing video games in person with friends on a daily or weekly basis. They also often play video games with their parents!

And they're not just playing together—they're *talking*. A majority of teen boys say they use online voice connections so they can talk and chat with their friends while playing. Think of a video game as the modern equivalent of a chessboard or pick-up game of basketball.

No Easy Verdict on Video Games

While there may be social benefits to playing video games, it is clear there are very real concerns about its effect on people's health. The best way to combat these risks is to keep playing time at a minimum. Use the ESRB ratings to help choose games that are rated appropriately for players' ages. Set limits for the amount of time spent gaming each day. Play for 30 minutes or an hour.

Then go do something that engages another part of the brain, such as working on a puzzle or drawing something.

Every parent has told a gaming child, "Get outside, go kick a ball around, shoot some hoops," and it's good advice. You might be able to perform a more amazing skateboard jump in a video game, but you can actually experience a *real* jump on a skateboard if you go outside. Read a fantasy adventure or a graphic novel. Or how about studying for that test next week?

Do anything that doesn't involve staring at a screen. We don't have to quit playing video games entirely. But it's time for us to try for the high score in other aspects of life.

Smart Technology Requires Smart Users

Today, more than 3 billion people around the world access the Internet, and almost 30,000 gigabytes of data travels over the Internet every second. We live in a digital age of constant wonder and amazement. It seems that every day brings new ways to keep in touch with loved ones, get our work done, and have fun.

Modern technology has disrupted many aspects of our lives by changing the way we normally do things. These disruptions can be positive, such as increasing the ease and efficiency of communication. But the disruptions also can be negative. We may love our smartphones and mobile devices because they provide us with instant access to information and help us organize our lives. But how do these devices, which have been found to be serious distractions, affect our ability to think and form memories? What new stresses do these devices place on our families, even as they help us keep in touch and stay organized? How does the time we spend online, whether on social media sites or playing video games, affect our social skills and health?

As the digital world continues to evolve, it's up to all of us to stay informed and engaged so that we understand how our interactions with technology affect our society, relationships, and health. The questions and arguments addressed in this book represent only a small fraction of the issues we face as digital citizens in an ever-evolving online landscape. There are no easy answers to these questions. Each of us must evaluate the benefits, and each of us must decide the potential risks we are willing to accept.

Images:

4–5: Vladgrin/Shutterstock; **6Bkgd:** Vladgrin/Shutterstock; **7:** LLL Photo/Alamy; **8:** PureSolution/Shutterstock; **11:** Jesadaphorn/Shutterstock; **12–13:** Jesadaphorn/Shutterstock; **14–15:** Restyler/Shutterstock; **17:** Olga Lebedeva/Shutterstock; **18–19:** Annette Shaff/Shutterstock; **20:** Monkey Business/Fotolia; **20–21Bkgd:** Petch one/Shutterstock; **21:** Mark Adams/123RF; **22:** Jesadaphorn/Shutterstock; **24–25:** Wong Yu Liang /123RF; **26:** Freightliner/Rex/AP Images; **31:** Rinspeed/Rex/AP Images; **32–33:** Jesadaphorn/Shutterstock; **35:** Dmitry Lemon5ky/Shutterstock; **38:** Macrovector/Shutterstock; **43:** Maximillion1/Shutterstock; **44:** Lisa F. Young/Shutterstock; **45:** Cathy Yeulet/123RF; **46–47:** Vladgrin/Shutterstock